D0090308

Congratulations,
by the way

CONGRATU-LATIONS, BY THE WAY

Some Thoughts on Kindness

GEORGE SAUNDERS

Illustrations by Chelsea Cardinal

RANDOM HOUSE
NEW YORK

Published in the United States by Random House, an imprint
and division of Random House LLC,
a Penguin Random House Company, New York.

RANDOM HOUSE and the HOUSE colophon are registered
trademarks of Random House LLC.

This is a slightly expanded version of a commencement speech
given by the author at Syracuse University, May 11, 2013.

ISBN 978-0-8129-9627-2
eBook ISBN 978-0-8129-9628-9

Printed in the United States of America on acid-free paper

www.atrandom.com

246897531

First Edition

Designed by Chelsea Cardinal

In loving memory of my grandparents:
John and Jane Clarke
George A. and Marie (Mae) Saunders

Congratulations,
by the way

DOWN THROUGH THE AGES, a traditional form has evolved for this type of speech, which is: Some old fart, his best years behind him, who over the course of his life has made a series of dreadful mistakes (that would be me), gives heartfelt advice to a group of shining, energetic young people with all of their best years ahead of them (that would be you).

And I intend to respect that tradition.

Now, one useful thing you can do with old people, in addition to borrowing money from them or getting them to do one of their old-time "dances," so you can watch while laughing, is ask, "Looking back, what do you regret?" And they'll tell you. Sometimes, as you know, they'll tell you even if you haven't asked. Sometimes, even when you've specifically requested that they not tell you, they'll tell you. So: What do I regret? Being poor from time to time? Not really. Working terrible jobs, like "knuckle-puller in a slaughterhouse"? (And don't even *ask* what that entails.) No. I don't regret that.

Skinny-dipping in a river in Sumatra, a little buzzed, and looking up and seeing like three hundred monkeys sitting on a pipeline, pooping down into the river, the river in which I was swimming, with my mouth open, naked? And getting deathly ill afterward, and staying sick for the next seven months? Honestly, no. Do I regret the occasional humiliation? Like once, playing hockey in front of a big crowd, including this girl I really liked, I somehow managed, while falling and emitting this weird whooping noise, to score on my own goalie, while also sending my stick flying into the crowd, nearly hitting that girl? No. I don't even regret that.

But here's something I do regret:

In seventh grade, this new kid joined our class. In the interest of confidentiality, her Convocation Speech name will be "ELLEN." ELLEN was small, shy. She wore these blue cat's-eye glasses that, at the time, only old ladies wore. When nervous, which was pretty much always, she had a habit of taking a strand of hair into her mouth and chewing on it.

So she came to our school and our neighborhood and was mostly ignored, occasionally teased. ("Your hair taste good?"—that sort of thing.) I could see this hurt her. I still remember the way she'd look after such an insult: eyes cast down, a little gut-kicked, as if, having just been reminded of her place in things, she was trying, as much as possible, to disappear. After a while she'd drift away, hair strand still in her mouth. At home, I imagined, after school, her mother would say, you know, "How was your day, sweetie?" and she'd say, "Oh, fine." And her mother would say, "Making any friends?" and she'd go, "Sure, lots."

Sometimes I'd see her hanging around alone in her front yard, as if afraid to leave it.

And then—they moved. That was it. No tragedy, no big final hazing.

One day she was there, next day she wasn't.

End of story.

Now, why do I regret *that*? Why, forty-two years later, am I still thinking about it? Relative to most of the other kids, I was actually pretty *nice* to her. I never said an unkind word to her. In fact, I sometimes even (mildly) defended her.

But still. It bothers me.

So here's something I know to be true, although it's a little corny, and I don't quite know what to do with it:

What I regret most in my life are *failures of kindness.*

Those moments when another human being was there, in front of me, suffering and I responded ... sensibly. Reservedly. Mildly.

Or, to look at it from the other end of the telescope: Who, in your life, do you remember most fondly, with the most undeniable feelings of warmth?

Those who were kindest to you, I bet.

It's a little facile, maybe, and certainly hard to implement, but I'd say, as a goal in life, you could do worse than: *Try to be kinder.*

Now, the million-dollar question: What's our problem—why aren't we kinder?

Here's what I think:

Each of us is born with a series of built-in confusions that are probably somehow Darwinian. These are: (1) we're central to the universe (that is, our personal story is the main and most interesting story, the *only* story, really); (2) we're separate from the universe (there's *us* and then, out there, all that other junk—dogs and swing sets and the state of Nebraska and low-hanging clouds and, you know, other people); and (3) we're permanent (death is real, okay, sure—for you, but not for me).

Now, we don't really believe these things—
intellectually, we know better—but we believe
them viscerally, and live by them, and they cause
us to prioritize our own needs over the needs of
others, even though what we really want, in our
hearts, is to be less selfish, more aware of what's
actually happening in the present moment, more
open, and more loving.

We know we want to be these things because
from time to time we *have been* these things—
and liked it.

So, the second million-dollar question: How might we *do* this? How might we become more loving, more open, less selfish, more present, less delusional, et cetera, et cetera?

Well, yes, good question.

Unfortunately, I only have three minutes left.

So let me just say this: There *are* ways. You already know that because, in your life, there have been High Kindness periods and Low Kindness periods, and you know what inclined you toward the former and away from the latter. It's an exciting idea: Since we have observed that kindness is *variable*, we might also sensibly conclude that it is *improvable;* that is, there must be approaches and practices that can actually increase our ambient level of kindness.

Education is good; immersing ourselves in a work of art: good; prayer is good; meditation's good; a frank talk with a dear friend; establishing ourselves in some kind of spiritual tradition—recognizing that there have been countless really smart people before us who have asked these same questions and left behind answers for us. It would be strange and self-defeating to fail to seek out these wise voices from the past—as self-defeating as it would be to attempt to rediscover the principles of physics from scratch or invent a new method of brain surgery without having learned the ones that already exist.

Because kindness, it turns out, is hard—it starts out all rainbows and puppy dogs and expands to include . . . well, everything.

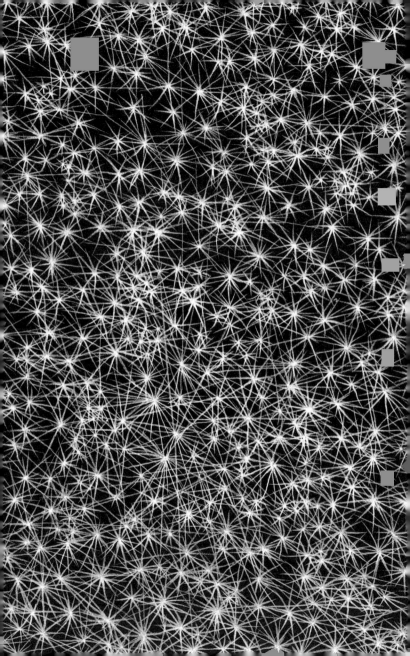

One thing in our favor: Some of this "becoming kinder" happens naturally, with age. It might be a simple matter of attrition: As we get older, we come to see how useless it is to be selfish—how illogical, really. We come to love certain other people and are thereby counterinstructed in our own centrality. We get our butts kicked by real life, and people come to our defense, and help us, and we learn that we're not separate, and don't want to be. We see people near and dear to us dropping away, and are gradually convinced that maybe we too will drop away (someday, a long time from now). Most people, as they age, become less selfish and more loving. I think this is true. The great Syracuse poet Hayden Carruth said, in a poem written near the end of his life, that he was mostly Love, now.

And so, a prediction, and my heartfelt wish for you: As you get older, your self will diminish and you will grow in love. YOU will gradually be replaced by LOVE. If you have kids, that will be a huge moment in your process of self-diminishment. You really won't care what happens to YOU, as long as they benefit. That's one reason your parents are so proud and happy today. One of their fondest dreams has come true: You have accomplished something difficult and tangible that has enlarged you as a person and will make your life better, from here on in, forever.

Congratulations, by the way.

When young, we're anxious—understandably—to find out if we've got what it takes. Can we succeed? Can we build a viable life for ourselves? But you—in particular you, of this generation—may have noticed a certain cyclical quality to ambition. You do well in high school, in the hopes of getting into a good college, so you can do well in the good college, in the hopes of getting a good job, so you can do well in the good job, so you can . . .

And this is actually okay. If we're going to become kinder, that process has to include taking ourselves seriously—as doers, as accomplishers, as dreamers. We have to do that, to be our best selves.

Still, accomplishment is unreliable. "Succeeding," whatever that might mean to you, is hard, and the need to do so constantly renews itself (success is like a mountain that keeps growing ahead of you as you hike it), and there's the very real danger that "succeeding" will take up your whole life, while the big questions go untended.

I can look back and see that I've spent much of my life in a cloud of things that have tended to push "being kind" to the periphery. Things like: Anxiety. Fear. Insecurity. Ambition. The mistaken belief that enough accomplishment will rid me of all that anxiety, fear, insecurity, and ambition. The belief that if I can only *accrue* enough— enough accomplishment, money, fame—my neuroses will disappear. I've been in this fog certainly since, at least, my own graduation day. Over the years I've felt: Kindness, sure—but first let me finish this semester, this degree, this book; let me succeed at this job, and afford this house, and raise these kids, and then, finally, when all is accomplished, I'll get started on the kindness. Except it never all gets accomplished. It's a cycle that can go on . . . well, forever.

So, quick, end-of-speech advice. Since, according to me, your life is going to be a gradual process of becoming kinder and more loving: Hurry up. Speed it along. Start right now. There's a confusion in each of us, a sickness, really: selfishness. But there's also a cure.

Be a good and proactive and even somewhat desperate patient on your own behalf—seek out the most efficacious anti-selfishness medicines, energetically, for the rest of your life. Find out what makes you kinder, what opens you up and brings out the most loving, generous, and unafraid version of you—and go after those things as if nothing else matters.

Because, actually, nothing else does.

Do all the other things, of course, the ambitious things—travel, get rich, get famous, innovate, lead, fall in love, make and lose fortunes, swim naked in wild jungle rivers (after first having them tested for monkey poop)—but as you do, to the extent that you can, *err in the direction of kindness*. Do those things that incline you toward the big questions, and avoid the things that would reduce you and make you trivial. That luminous part of you that exists beyond personality—your soul, if you will—is as bright and shining as any that has ever been. Bright as Shakespeare's, bright as Gandhi's, bright as Mother Teresa's. Clear away everything that keeps you separate from this secret, luminous place. Believe that it exists, come to know it better, nurture it, share its fruits tirelessly.

And someday, in eighty years, when you're a hundred and I'm a hundred and thirty-four, and we're both so kind and loving we're nearly unbearable, drop me a line, let me know how your life has been. I hope you will say: It has been so wonderful.

I wish you great happiness, all the luck in the world, and a beautiful summer.

ABOUT THE AUTHOR

GEORGE SAUNDERS is the author of seven previous books, including the story collections *Tenth of December* and *Pastoralia*. He has received fellowships from the Lannan Foundation, the American Academy of Arts and Letters, and the Guggenheim Foundation. In 2006 he was awarded a MacArthur Fellowship. In 2013 he was awarded the PEN/Malamud Award for Excellence in the Short Story and was included in *Time*'s list of the 100 most influential people in the world. He teaches in the Creative Writing Program at Syracuse University.